GRAND CENTRAL TERMINAL

GATEWAY TO NEW YORK CITY

ED STANLEY

THE AUTHOR GRATEFULLY ACKNOWLEDGES THE EXPERTISE
AND KIND SUPPORT OF JOHN TAURANAC.

❋ ❋ ❋

TEXT COPYRIGHT © 2003 BY MONDO PUBLISHING

MAPS ON PP. 8 AND 19 DESIGNED BY JOHN TAURANAC © TAURANAC, LTD., 2003

PHOTOGRAPHY AND ILLUSTRATION CREDITS:

Every effort has been made to trace the ownership of all copyright materials in this book
and to obtain permission for their use.
Front cover, pp. 4, 25: © Peter Aaron/Esto; back cover, pp. 9 (top), 26 (top right), 31, 43 (bottom): © Frank
English/MTA Metro-North Railroad; p. 26 (left): Courtesy NYC Municipal Archives; pp. 3, 30, 42 (bottom), 43 (top),
44 (right): Photographs by James Rudnick ©; pp. 9 (bottom), 10 (top right), 35 (top right), 40: © Bettmann/CORBIS;
p. 10 (left): Collections of The New York Public Library, Astor, Lenox and Tilden Foundations; pp. 11, 33 (bottom):
Collection of The Library of Congress; p. 12 (top): Courtesy *Scientific American*, February 15, 1890 ed.; pp. 12
(bottom), 13, 15, 33, 35 (top left): Courtesy of New York Transit Museum; pp. 14, 23, 27: Collection of The New-York
Historical Society; p. 17: Courtesy The Donald Duke Collection; p. 20: William Wilgus Papers, Manuscripts and
Archives Division, The New York Public Library, Astor, Lenox and Tilden Foundations; p. 22: Courtesy *Scientific
American*, December 7, 1912 ed.; pp. 28-29: Courtesy Avery Architectural and Fine Arts Library, Columbia University
in the City of New York; p. 32: © Frank Fournier/Contact Press Images/PictureQuest; p. 34: © CORBIS; p. 35 (bottom):
© K. Thichenor/ Robertstock.com; p. 36: Courtesy Gurney Family Trust; p. 37: © Laura Rosen; p. 38: © Museum of
the City of New York; p. 39: © Neal Boenzi/The New York Times; p. 41: © Beyer Blinder Belle Architects & Planners,
James W. Rhodes photographer, from *Grand Central Terminal: Gateway to a Million Lives* by John Belle & Maxinne R.
Leighton; p. 42 (top): © Ross Muir; p. 44 (left): © Beyer Blinder Belle Architects & Planners, Anne Edris photographer,
from *Grand Central Terminal: Gateway to a Million Lives* by John Belle & Maxinne R. Leighton

FOR INFORMATION CONTACT

MONDO PUBLISHING 980 AVENUE OF THE AMERICAS, NEW YORK, NY 10018
VISIT OUR WEB SITE AT http://www.mondopub.com
PRINTED IN CHINA

03 04 05 06 07 08   9 8 7 6 5 4 3 2 1

ISBN 1-59034-491-X (HC)   ISBN 1-59034-492-8 (PB)

COVER AND BOOK DESIGN BY MICHELLE FARINELLA

LIBRARY OF CONGRESS CATALOGING-IN-PUBLICATION DATA

Stanley, Ed.
     Grand Central Terminal : gateway to New York City / Ed Stanley.
          p. cm.
     Includes index.
     Summary: Provides a history of Grand Central Terminal from the mid-
nineteenth century to the present, including its construction and architecture,
the role played by Cornelius Vanderbilt, and facts about railroads in general.
     Contents: The Commodore's empire -- An enormous problem, a brilliant solution --
A gigantic construction project -- New York City's triumphal gateway -- From triumph
to tragedy -- A train station for the 21st century -- Time line.
     ISBN 1-59034-491-X -- ISBN 1-59034-492-8 (pbk.)
Grand Central Terminal (New York, NY)--History--Juvenile literature. 2. Railroad terminals--
New York (State)--New York--History--Juvenile literature. [1. Grand Central Terminal
(New York, NY)--History. 2. Railroad stations.] I. Title.

TF302.N7 S73 2003
385.3'14'097471--dc21

2002190719

CONTENTS

INTRODUCTION

THE NEXT TIME you are in New York City (if you are not already there), go to Park Avenue between 46th and 50th Streets. Turn onto one of those side streets and look down through a sidewalk grate. What you will see are railroad tracks. The story of how they got there is the story of what some have called one of the greatest engineering and architectural miracles of our time. That miracle is GRAND CENTRAL TERMINAL.

But, you say, Grand Central Terminal is a building, and the building is on 42nd Street. And you would be absolutely right—except for the fact that Grand Central Terminal is so much more than a building. The ancestors of those tracks you saw through the grate ran at street level right through the middle of Manhattan at the end of the 19th century. An enormous train yard split the city in half for eight blocks. Living on Park Avenue, then called Fourth Avenue, was a lot like living alongside a blast furnace. It was certainly no park.

There were a lot of problems with the old Grand Central Station, which was really neither grand nor central. Unfortunately, as often happens, it took a crisis to get the attention of the people in power and force them to solve those problems. The Grand Central Terminal that we know today was born from the ashes of a tragic train wreck.

Now the name is perfect. Architecturally speaking, the building is a grand space—grand in every sense, but at the same time warm and user-friendly. More about that later. Central, because it's at the heart and center of New York City, although this was not always the case. More about that later, too. And terminal, not station, because every train that arrives there, terminates there. It is not a "through station," it's a destination, the end of the line. An old joke tells of an upstate New York farmer on his way to the big city for the first time. "Say," he addressed the conductor nervously, "does this train stop in New York City?" The conductor looked at him, pondering his response. "Gonna be an awful crash if it don't," he finally replied.

So it is the building, Grand Central Terminal, that you may first think of when you hear the name. In terms of area, the terminal extends seven stories into the air and five stories below ground. Its property extends from 42nd Street north to 50th Street, and from Madison Avenue east to Lexington Avenue—48 acres of incredibly valuable land. But it is the continuing story behind the building—the story of a rapidly growing city, powerful men and women, brilliant architects and engineers, and the golden age of long-distance train travel and its subsequent decline—that gives meaning to the building itself. And best of all, it is a story with a happy ending.

Remember the sidewalk grate? Think of it as a window into an amazing world—a city within a city—that changed New York forever.

OUR STORY BEGINS UNDERGROUND,
JUST LIKE THOSE RAILROAD TRACKS.
READ ON.

CHAPTER ONE

THE COMMODORE'S EMPIRE

✳ THE CRASH ✳

THE MORNING OF January 8, 1902, was a frigid one. Engineer John Wiskar's rush-hour train from upstate New York was running late, but his destination—New York City's Grand Central Station—was almost in sight. The entrance to the Park Avenue tunnel lay just ahead. All trains bound for Grand Central had to pass through the two-mile (3.2 km) tunnel. At this time of day, the trains, pulled by steam engines, entered the tunnel at a rate of about one train every 45 seconds.

At the other end of the tunnel, a commuter train from Connecticut was held up due to the usual train-yard congestion. So the signalman posted a green semaphore inside the tunnel that meant "proceed with caution." He then turned the next signal, a large red semaphore meaning "danger," into position.

According to railroad rules, a flare had to be placed on the track, too. It would go off automatically if a train ran the signal. Detonation of the flare would even sound a loud gong! So the flagman set the flare and then stood by with a glowing red lantern in either hand, just in case.

Engineer Wiskar's train entered the dark, smoky tunnel at 96th Street. He approached the green semaphore that required him to

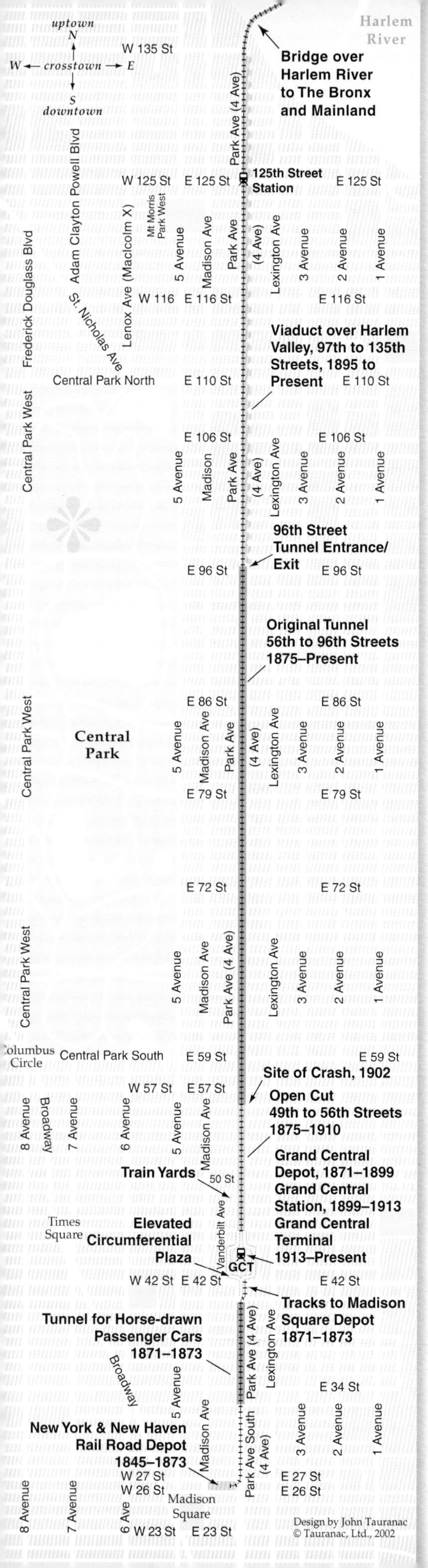
uptown
N
W ← crosstown → E
S
downtown
Harlem River
Bridge over Harlem River to The Bronx and Mainland
W 135 St
Park Ave (4 Ave)
Frederick Douglass Blvd
Adam Clayton Powell Blvd
W 125 St
E 125 St
125th Street Station
E 125 St
Lenox Ave (Maclcolm X)
Mt Morris Park West
5 Avenue
Madison Ave
Park Ave
(4 Ave)
Lexington Ave
3 Avenue
2 Avenue
1 Avenue
St. Nicholas Ave
W 116
E 116 St
E 116 St
Viaduct over Harlem Valley, 97th to 135th Streets, 1895 to Present
Central Park North
E 110 St
E 110 St
Central Park West
E 106 St
E 106 St
96th Street Tunnel Entrance/ Exit
E 96 St
E 96 St
Original Tunnel 56th to 96th Streets 1875–Present
E 86 St
E 86 St
Central Park
E 79 St
E 79 St
E 72 St
E 72 St
Park Ave (4 Ave)
Columbus Circle
Central Park South
E 59 St
E 59 St
Site of Crash, 1902
W 57 St
E 57 St
Open Cut 49th to 56th Streets 1875–1910
8 Avenue
Broadway
7 Avenue
6 Avenue
Grand Central Depot, 1871–1899
Grand Central Station, 1899–1913
Grand Central Terminal 1913–Present
Train Yards
50 St
Vanderbilt Ave
Times Square
Elevated Circumferential Plaza
GCT
W 42 St
E 42 St
E 42 St
Tracks to Madison Square Depot 1871–1873
Tunnel for Horse-drawn Passenger Cars 1871–1873
Broadway
E 34 St
New York & New Haven Rail Road Depot 1845–1873
Park Ave South (4 Ave)
W 27 St
W 26 St
E 27 St
E 26 St
Madison Square
6 Ave
W 23 St
E 23 St
Design by John Tauranac
© Tauranac, Ltd., 2002

proceed with caution. But the train sped right by, causing his fireman to call out, "Green! Green!" Wiskar never heard the fireman.

The danger signal came into view of the fireman, but not, evidently, the engineer. "Red! Red!" yelled the fireman as the train thundered on. The flare discharged. The gong sounded—and still the train rushed onward. When the flagman standing at trackside realized that the train was continuing at normal speed despite all of the signals, he frantically smashed both of his lanterns against the front of the engine as it sped by—to no avail. Seconds later, Wiskar's train plunged into the rear of the Connecticut train, instantly killing 15 people. Two more died days later, and many others were injured. It was the worst railroad accident ever in Manhattan.

The public was furious. The tunnel was a notorious health and safety hazard. It had spewed steam and cinders into the surrounding neighborhood for years. As a result of the crash, a law was passed that required the railroad to get rid of steam engines and substitute electric ones (a fairly new technology) by July 1, 1908.

The splendid Grand Central Terminal that we know today was the direct result of that law. We'll see just how in Chapter Two. But how had it come to this? What were the makings of the tragedy? To answer these questions, we need to take a look at a bit of railroad history and at one man in particular—"Commodore" Cornelius Vanderbilt.

This map of a part of the island of Manhattan shows the railroad's route to and from Grand Central, along with other historical notations and points of interest.

☀ THE "COMMODORE" ☀

A bronze statue of Cornelius Vanderbilt stands on a pedestal in front of today's Grand Central Terminal. It was Vanderbilt who built the original Grand Central in 1871. No doubt he would approve of the pedestal.

When Vanderbilt died in 1877, he was the richest man in America. Born in 1794, he was a farm boy and a mediocre student who left school at the age of 11. Vanderbilt made his fortune in the steamboat business, where he acquired his nickname, the "Commodore." He'd gone into business with one small sailing boat at the age of 16. By the 1850s he ran a huge shipping empire that was worth millions. And he took a dim view of the upstart railroad industry—the new kid on the block.

The statue of Vanderbilt in front of Grand Central Terminal's main entrance is larger than life-size.

But Vanderbilt changed his mind when he was about 70 years old—an age when many might decide to retire. It became clear to him that America's westward expansion would depend mostly on steel rails, not waterways. He foresaw the coming of the age of railroads and knew there were fortunes to be made. Unable to resist, he decided to put together another empire. By 1869 he had acquired three railroads. His new empire, the New York Central Railroad, would become the greatest American railroad empire of the 19th century.

Once Vanderbilt had his empire, it was obvious that he needed a suitable passenger terminal.

Cornelius Vanderbilt (1794–1877)

This political cartoon from 1870 depicts Vanderbilt as a railroad baron.

He decided something resembling a palace would do. It would be built on land that was a combination of railroad property at 42nd Street and Fourth Avenue and an adjoining 23 acres that he had quietly acquired.

Vanderbilt's choice of location was at the very edge of the city, right next to undesirable things, like breweries and slaughterhouses.

Trains had to be pulled by horses from 42nd Street south to the 26th Street terminal.

His decision was laughed at, but it made sense. The steam engines that pulled trains in those days had been banned south of 42nd Street. Local residents hated the noisy, dirty locomotives that chugged through the city right on the streets, belching smoke in all directions and occasionally running over an unfortunate pedestrian or two. So by the end of 1858, trains had to be decoupled at 42nd Street and pulled by horses south to the terminal at 26th Street. Why build a railroad palace where steam engines couldn't even go?

True, in 1869, 42nd Street was a long way from the heart of the city. Some called it "the end of the Earth." But Vanderbilt predicted the growth of the city northward up the slender island of Manhattan. He felt that the city would soon overtake and continue right on past his 42nd Street property—making the location exactly central. Which is just what happened.

❊ THE DEPOT ❊

Grand Central Depot, 1871

Vanderbilt's Grand Central Depot opened in 1871. In addition to the palatial head house, it had an amazing arched train shed of iron and glass. The enormous shed could hold 15,000 people and about 100 train cars at one time. The depot's fancy Victorian façade, or front, looked to the south toward the city proper. The ugly rear of the train shed and the smoky train yards faced the outskirts to the north.

The train shed was kept fairly quiet and smoke-free using some unusual methods. One was the infamous "flying switch"—designed to keep incoming steam locomotives out of the shed. Here's how it worked: As a train heading for the depot emerged from the Park Avenue tunnel, the engineer would shut down the steam. The brake-man, precariously perched over the coupler that linked the engine to the first car, would release the coupler, yell out, and wave his right hand. The engineer would then throw on as much steam as he could and drive the now released engine full-steam ahead to a

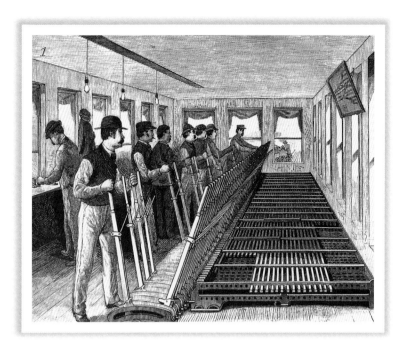

Each track had its own towerman. When a train approached a track alongside the shed, the towerman for that track would throw the switch back and direct the train into the shed.

track alongside the shed. A towerman who was watching closely would throw the switch back just in time to direct the rest of the train (now rolling along on its own momentum, without its engine) into the train shed. Brakemen onboard then turned the handbrakes furiously in order to stop alongside the passenger platform inside the shed. Amazingly, no serious accidents were ever recorded from this split-second maneuver.

The train shed enclosed the largest interior space in North America– 200 feet wide, 100 feet high, and over 600 feet long (61 m by 30.5 m by almost 200 m).

✳ THE TUNNEL ✳

The railroad's route to the depot ran along Fourth Avenue, right at street level. Noise and smoke made it an environmental nightmare. So by 1875 the tracks were lowered into an "open cut" from 49th Street to 56th Street. From 56th to 96th Streets, the tracks were placed in a "ventilated" tunnel.

Then, a landscaped strip of garden plots was built to serve as a lid to the tunnel. Fourth Avenue, now Park Avenue, became wider and more desirable. The garden plots framed the vents that were supposed to keep the tunnel smoke-free. Unfortunately, the vents acted more like chimneys, directing volcanic eruptions of smoke and cinders into the faces of pedestrians. The vents did little to clear the tunnel.

The City insisted that the railroad lower its tracks into a partially covered channel or "open cut."

✳ THE STATION ✳

By the late 1880s, waves of immigrants were landing on Manhattan's shores, and the population of the city and its suburbs was increasing rapidly. Passenger volume on New York railroads tripled between

Grand Central Station was topped off with four domed clock towers flanked by stone eagles with 13-foot (4 m) wingspans.

1871 and the end of the 19th century. By 1898, over 500 trains operated to and from Grand Central every weekday. Many were commuter trains from developing suburbs.

Completely unequipped to handle the load, the Commodore's Depot was radically renovated in 1898. A three-story addition, an enlarged concourse, a rebuilt waiting-room area, and an expanded train yard tried to deal with the crowds. The new and the old exteriors together were covered over with fake stone. The resulting six-story extravaganza was now called Grand Central Station.

The interior was reorganized to eliminate congestion and improve traffic flow. But still the station swarmed with travelers. A new state-of-the-art switching system, meant to replace the flying switch, ended up causing long delays instead. There simply were not enough tracks

Dead-end tracks in the crowded, smoke-filled train yard required trains to back up and turn in order to exit, which caused congestion and delays.

to handle the traffic. Trains were often held up as they emerged from the tunnel, causing dangerous back-ups. The renovated Grand Central Station was inadequate almost from the day it was finished. Critics called it the worst rail facility in the country. New Yorkers complained more and more about the open train yards and tracks that created a filthy, noisy barrier to crosstown traffic that extended all the way from 42nd to 56th Streets.

AND THEN

CAME THE CRASH.

CHAPTER TWO

AN ENORMOUS PROBLEM, A BRILLIANT SOLUTION

☀ THE ENGINEER ☀

YOU'VE PROBABLY HEARD the expression "Necessity is the mother of invention." It means that things usually get invented because there is a need for them. As a result of the crash, an electrified railroad was needed. But inventions often need a father as well as a mother. The father of the solution to this problem was William J. Wilgus—a brilliant young civil engineer. Remember the railroad tracks we saw through the sidewalk grate on Park Avenue? That was Wilgus's idea. That—and so much more.

☀ THE PROBLEM ☀

Electrifying the New York Central Railroad, which would cost a lot of money, was not the only problem. The terminal building was hopelessly overcrowded. The train yards were a clogged nightmare of dead-end tracks. The entire situation was awkward, inefficient, and, as we have seen, increasingly dangerous. As the "Commodore" had predicted, New York had grown uptown. Grand Central was now situated near the heart of it all. As train traffic continued to increase at an astounding rate, it was clear that the terminal needed to grow. But how? Where?

The solution had to be one that would stand the test of time. It would require someone with vision—someone who could foresee, as the "Commodore" had, how things would play out in years to come. William J. Wilgus had both the vision and the genius to solve the problem. He is one of New York City's great unsung heroes.

✳ THE SOLUTION ✳

Wilgus's plan was complicated and expensive. Rather than expand horizontally, which was impossible, Grand Central would expand vertically—up and (mostly) down. And what's more, the expansion would help pay for itself in the end.

Vertical expansion was possible because electric trains don't require open air for ventilation like steam engines do. Electric trains can run underground. Not only that—thanks to the new building technology that brought us skyscrapers (steel-frame construction), tracks could be built in two layers, one over another—just like floors in a building.

William J. Wilgus, Chief Engineer

HERE IS WHAT WILGUS PROPOSED:

1. Tear down the entire Grand Central complex south of 56th Street.

2. Build a 57-track, all electric, two-level underground train yard—then cover it up. (Remember, electrification meant that the railroad yard and tracks could now be completely covered.)

3. Include two looping tracks on each level, allowing trains to circle

around and pick up departing passengers after letting out the arriving ones, or just circle around and go for maintenance—no backing up required.

4. Design and erect an entirely new terminal building.

5. Restore Park Avenue and all of the crosstown streets that had been interrupted by the old train yard.

6. Lease air rights to help pay for it.

Air rights? Exactly. The railroad would literally pull money out of the air. Once Park Avenue was paved over, the railroad could lease newly-created building sites on this now important thoroughfare. Developers who leased these sites could erect buildings right over the concealed tracks. Since the railroad owned the land, they could even have some say in the design of these buildings so that the resulting Terminal City, as Wilgus called it, would be harmonious and elegant. That was the idea, anyway.

Of course, the buildings would have no basements. They would have railroad tracks in their cellars. Steel beams and columns buried deep in bedrock and rising between the railroad tracks would hold the buildings up—and the railroad would collect rent. A lot of it. Since Wilgus's project was estimated to cost $80 million (about $2 billion today), the leasing of air rights was a crucial part of the plan.

The solution was accepted unanimously. All that was required now was a plan to implement the solution. And who better to design it than William J. Wilgus? For this was no simple construction project.

1. Pull down all of the old facilities and cart away the debris.

2. Excavate 48 acres of earth and (mostly) rock (194,249 sq m or 46 football fields worth) in the heart of New York City down to about 45 feet (13.7 m)—and then haul it all away.

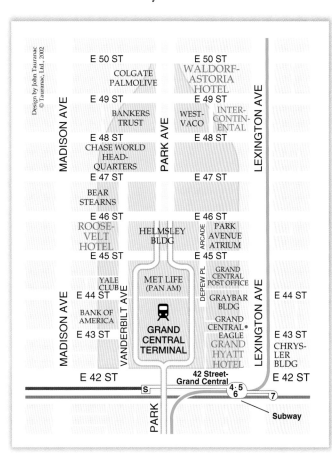

3. Erect a double-decker track system and lay 32 miles (51.5 km) of track.

4. Restore all the original streets.

5. Erect a new terminal building.

6. Do it all with absolutely *no interruption* to train service in and out of Grand Central—which, in 1903, was about 600 trains a day and increasing rapidly.

The darker shaded area on the map shows where tracks lie underground–in the basements of the hotels, apartments, and office buildings built over them.

   Remember, there was a deadline—July 1, 1908. Construction began on July 18, 1903.

COULD THEY PULL IT OFF

IN JUST FIVE YEARS?

CHAPTER THREE

A GIGANTIC CONSTRUCTION PROJECT

※ ELECTRICITY COMES
TO GRAND CENTRAL ※

THEY COULD—and they did. On September 30, 1906, a brand new electric engine made its first run to Grand Central. Wilgus himself was at the controls. He'd had a minor problem along the way—a 1,000 foot (304.8 m) gap in the electrified third rail that powered the train. But never mind—he just stepped on the "gas" and let speed carry him right over the gap. Regular service on electric trains began about three months later, and by July 1907, almost all of the New York Central's trains were powered by electricity.

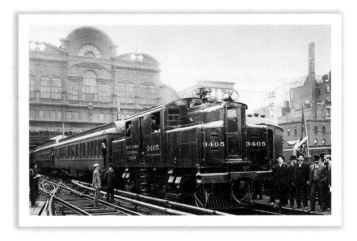

Wilgus drove the first electric train engine to arrive at Grand Central. It got there a full year ahead of the deadline.

It was an incredible accomplishment. In just four years, Wilgus and his team had completely replaced the loud, smoky steam engines with clean, quiet electric ones, using a system they designed and tested. Even more amazing was the fact that this was only one small piece of the massive project Wilgus was in charge of.

The organized and methodical Wilgus had divided the entire undertaking into eight monumental projects. Electrification was just one. Next came excavation of the train yard; construction of the two-story underground track system; and construction of the new Grand Central Terminal building. Once again, Wilgus proved to be the person with the solution.

Take a look back on page 19 at what had to be done. The toughest part would be pulling it off without any interruption to train service. Traffic in the overcrowded station increased every year during the construction project. How could they keep 750,000 passengers moving in and out each weekday while building a whole new system? Wilgus planned the construction in a series of three "bites." The bites moved from east to west. As one was finished, the next would be started.

HERE'S WHAT WOULD HAPPEN IN EACH BITE:

1. All buildings within the bite would be demolished and any existing tracks removed.

2. Workers would excavate the bite to about 45 feet deep (13.7 m) (more or less in some places).

3. Construction workers would erect the steel frame that would support two levels of tracks and the streets above them. (Eventually, they would erect the frame of the new terminal building on the site of the old one.)

4. Concrete floors, walls, and ceilings would be poured.

5. New train platforms would be built.

6. Utilities, like water and drainpipes, would be installed.

The construction of the new terminal is in progress, with the new electrified system visible on the left and the old steam engines visible on the right. The excavation is going on in the middle.

7. New tracks would be laid, including the electrified third rail.

8. Switches and signals would be installed.

9. New tracks would be put into service and workmen would move on to the next bite.

And so the new would replace the old—gradually. Demolition for Bite 1 began in August of 1903.

✳ MORE PROBLEMS, MORE SOLUTIONS ✳

By the end of the project, about 2,000,000 cubic yards (1,529,109 cubic m) of rock and 1,250,000 cubic yards (995,693 cubic m) of earth—together, equal to the amount of concrete in the Hoover Dam—had been either dug out with steam shovels or blasted out with dynamite and removed by hand. Exhausted workmen used close to a million pounds (453,592 kg) of dynamite to blast through the tough bedrock. But how to get the rubble out of the way? In those days, work crews usually used horse-drawn wagons to clear construction sites. Each wagon held about four cubic yards (3.1 cubic m), which was fine for most normal jobs. But at that rate they would need over a million wagon loads for the Grand Central project! Clearly they'd need something more efficient.

To Wilgus the solution was obvious—use the railroad itself. So workmen used bucket hoists and steam shovels to fill the "hopper" cars, which carried debris through the Park Avenue tunnel and out of Manhattan. As work progressed from one bite to the next, crews just moved the

tracks over! Sometimes excavation would take place right alongside an existing building's foundation. The railroad would have to carefully shore up those foundation walls to be sure not to damage them. It was a tricky process.

Storage of supplies was another problem. Construction of the new train yard and terminal required 118,600 tons (107,592 metric tons) of steel and a million barrels of cement. A single steel beam might weigh as much as 88,000 pounds (39,916 kg). There was no way that all of this could be stored at or near the construction site. Getting it there required some planning. Again, the railroad provided the solution. All the steel was sorted and stored outside the city. Special twelve-car freight trains brought batches in during the night just before it would be needed.

Taking down the train shed was especially challenging. Remember, people were still using the train platforms inside it! Again, Wilgus and his team came up with a solution and, again, he used the railroad. They devised an enormous 100-foot-high (30.5 m) wooden scaffold that stretched from one side of the train shed to the other. It was curved, just like the shed roof, and it rested on train wheels. During the day, workmen high in the air took sections of the shed apart from the inside and placed them on the scaffold. At night the debris was

Demolishing the train shed meant taking down 1,700 tons (1,542,214 kg) of iron, 150 square feet (13,936 sq m) of roofing and glass, and half a million bricks!

lowered into freight cars and removed. The traveling scaffold then moved ahead to the next section of the train shed. It all worked without a hitch and without a single injury—and passengers kept right on using the platforms.

✳ A New Terminal Building ✳

When the last train left the old Grand Central on June 5, 1910, the

the new Grand Central Terminal, circa 1914

time had come to demolish and replace the "Commodore"'s palace. A competition for the design of the new terminal had taken place in 1903, with troubling results. Two architectural firms ended up sharing the project. Although this unhappy arrangement caused enormous delays, problems, and even a law suit, the terminal that emerged clearly represented the best that both firms had to offer. The glorious building that we know as Grand Central Terminal opened to the public at the stroke of midnight on February 2, 1913—just ten years after the project had begun. It was instantly beloved and acclaimed as perhaps the finest railroad terminal in the world—"a monumental gateway to America's greatest city."

For many people, Grand Central Terminal is a building and nothing more. Now that you know differently, it's time to have a look inside this extraordinary place.

Come.

CHAPTER FOUR

New York City's Triumphal Gateway

The Exterior

IF YOU WERE ENTERING a city in ancient times, the odds are that you would pass through an opening in the strong walls that surrounded and protected it. If the city was an important one, this opening was probably an elaborate triumphal archway, complete with statues and fancy details. The archway would have been massive and important-looking. When you passed through it, you'd have known you had *arrived*.

The architect Whitney Warren believed that modern cities needed gateways, too. He designed Grand Central Terminal to be New York City's triumphal gateway. He knew that he was designing the most important urban gateway ever created in this country, and he rose to the challenge. It is Warren who deserves the credit for the beauty of the terminal's interior and exterior. Whether you enter from the street or by train, you experience the same sensation. You know you have arrived!

His design called for not one but *three* huge arches on the main façade of Grand Central Terminal. The arches are 60 feet (18.3 m) high with pairs of columns on either side. And, since no triumphal archway was complete without some statuary, a 1,500 ton (1,361 metric ton) sculpture of Mercury, Hercules, and Minerva was added to celebrate the "glory of commerce."

The 50 foot (15.2 m) sculpture atop Grand Central's main façade includes a 13-foot (4 m) wide stained-glass clock.

A portion of Reed's "elevated circumferential plaza" shows Park Avenue wrapping around the terminal.

This imposing façade looks south, down Park Avenue, where most New Yorkers still lived and worked at the time it was built. But another architect, Charles Reed, gets the credit for deciding how to deal with Park Avenue where it bumped into the terminal. Rather than simply ending the street, only to have it continue on the other side of the building, or sending the street through the middle of the Main Concourse, Reed created an "elevated circumferential plaza." He simply split Park Avenue in half, lifted it up, and wrapped it around both sides of the building. Once it got around to the other side, its two halves came together and continued.

Looking at this sturdy building, you might think that those massive walls of granite and limestone are holding it up. But they're not. Grand Central Terminal was built using another technology that, like electricity, was relatively new at the time. The terminal has a steel frame, just like the skyscrapers that were beginning to sprout up all over Manhattan. The framework holds the building up, just as your skeleton holds you up. The stone walls, called curtain walls, just hang from the frame like curtains,

keeping out the rain and keeping in the warmth. Now, let's go inside.

The terminal's steel frame is anchored in bedrock. The walls do nothing to hold up the building.

✷ THE INTERIOR RAMPS ✷

Both Whitney Warren and Charles Reed believed it was important that a building's architecture respect its purpose. A writer for *Scientific American* stated it this way: "How to build a station so that John Smith or Mary Jones, who have never been in New York, can arrive at the Grand Central Terminal and pass through it to where he or she is going with the least possible confusion and the utmost . . . peace of mind." After all, this is what a train station has to do—help move passengers and their baggage quickly and easily either into or out of the city. When it opened in 1913, Grand Central Terminal was actually two stations in one. And both stations did exactly what they were supposed to do.

The stations were on two separate levels, just like the tracks. The upper level was for arriving and departing long-distance travelers, and the lower level was for suburban commuters. The long-distance arrival platform was soon dubbed the Kissing Gallery because of the affectionate reunions that took place there. Keeping all these passengers and their baggage moving easily to or from the building's 12 separate entrances without colliding or going around in circles was the challenge. Charles Reed's brilliant system of ramps throughout the terminal, originally thought up by Wilgus, was the solution. Not only did they work perfectly then, they still work perfectly today.

Wilgus and Reed both felt that ramps were the best way to move huge numbers of people efficiently. The plan to include them in Grand Central Terminal was the first time it had ever been done in America. Several temporary ramps were installed during construction, each with different degrees of slope, or slant. The architects observed carefully to see what worked best. They finally decided that the maximum slope should be a little less than 10%. So for every 100 feet (30.5 m) of length, the ramps rose about 8 feet (2.4 m). Of course, there are stairways and elevators in the terminal, too. But by using the ramps, it was possible to go from a taxi outside all the way to a seat on a train on either level without using a single stairway. It still is.

*cutaway drawing
of ramp system
inside the terminal*

✳ THE MAIN CONCOURSE ✳

It's been said that if you release a barrel right inside one of the entrances and let it roll down the ramps, it will arrive in the Main Concourse and stop right in front of a ticket window. While this has never been tried, it does seem like a possibility when you're inside the terminal. The Main Concourse is easy to find. The ramps just seem to take you there. And when you get there, you know once again that you have arrived. The concourse is breathtaking .

The floor is an acre of Tennessee marble. All the trim is marble, too. And the walls are a lovely, warm . . . fake stone. Well, it cost a lot less—and you'd never know it wasn't real. Many people have been fooled by its beauty! The three huge arched windows at either end are

one of Grand Central Terminal's many ramps

as big as those on the main façade. And right in the center of the concourse is the information booth. People have been meeting there, "under the clock," ever since the terminal opened. Inside the booth is a hidden spiral stair. If you climb down, you arrive inside the information booth on the lower level.

But the best part of the Main Concourse is overhead. There, on the vaulted ceiling 125 feet (38 m) up, is an astronomical mural complete with 2,500 stars. Sixty of them are lit up. The mural shows the constellations of the winter zodiac outlined in gold against a cerulean blue sky: Aquarius, Pisces, Aries, Taurus, Gemini, Cancer, plus Orion and Pegasus. Glorious.

But take another look. All but Orion are painted backwards! The East is in the West! How did this happen? While no one is positive, it's likely that the designer of the mural copied a medieval manuscript that showed the constellations from the point of view of the other side, looking back at the Earth. That was the medieval custom. It doesn't matter. The ceiling is beautiful.

✸ ELSEWHERE IN THE TERMINAL ✸

Services like information, ticket windows, and baggage checking were all in the Main Concourse. This meant that the Main Waiting Room remained a quiet place filled with amenities that made life pleasant for the traveler. Five huge bronze chandeliers that had a total of 720 light-bulbs hung from the 50-foot (15.2 m) ceiling. Grand Central was the first fully electrified train station in the country and electricity was still a new thing—so Warren wanted to show it off.

Another special feature of the terminal's interior was the vaulted ceilings of Guastavino tile. In what is called the Whispering Gallery on the ramps between the upper and lower concourses, a person can whisper into one corner of the tiled vault

The constellations on the ceiling are painted backwards.

and magically be heard by someone standing diagonally across in another corner. Your voice just skitters across the tile to the other side.

When the terminal opened, there were 75 clocks that you could see—and many more behind the scenes, that you couldn't see. All of these clocks—close to 150 in all—were cared for by one man for 50 years, Jake the Clockmeister.

He'd begin each day at 8:00 A.M. sharp, checking his watch in front of the master clock. Then he'd go outside to check his favorite clock,

*the great stained-glass clock, with the clockmeister
waving out the window*

the 13-foot (4 m) stained-glass one that is part of the sculpture on the main façade. From the street you can see a window in the clock face near the numeral VI. If the clock face needed servicing, that's how Jake reached the outside. He cleaned and oiled the clockworks twice a week, after climbing four separate ladders to get to it.

Grand Central Terminal was a success from the day it opened. In addition to the railroad facilities, its vast spaces have housed a post office, a newsreel movie theater, an emergency room, a police department, an art gallery, tennis courts, a private club, and more. People said you could live happily for days in the place without ever needing to go outside. There was even a tale (probably a tall one) of a fugitive from the police who hid for two years in the spaces and tunnels of Grand Central!

But some of the other Grand Central tales aren't a bit tall. Some are funny, others are amazing.

AND ONE IS VERY SAD.

the elegant Main Waiting Room, with its huge chandeliers, circa 1914

The Oyster Bar restaurant on the lower level of the terminal also has ceilings of Guastavino tile.

The Main Concourse was called "one of the grandest spaces the early 20th century ever enclosed," by architectural critic Paul Goldberger.

CHAPTER FIVE

FROM TRIUMPH TO TRAGEDY

※ RAILROAD'S GLORY DAYS ※

WHEN GRAND CENTRAL TERMINAL opened in 1913, it was more than the gateway to a growing New York City—it seemed to be the gateway to an entire continent. And the timing was perfect. Railroading was growing in popularity, and Grand Central became a symbol of the golden age of train travel.

The 20th Century Limited rocketed from Chicago to New York (or the reverse) in just 16 hours.

Every day the railroad literally rolled out the red carpet for the arrival or departure of the 20th Century Limited, one of the great limiteds that thrived during the days when trains were the most glamorous and luxurious way to travel. People crammed the terminal for the train's morning arrival in hopes of spotting a celebrity or two. If you were among the rich and famous, this was how you traveled. The railroad tried hard to throw off autograph seekers by not announcing the arrival gate until the last minute, but those "in the know" knew where to go. Arrivals were always a scene.

The 20th Century Limited was outfitted with plush seats, private sleeping cars with chairs and sofas, elegant dining cars, a barber shop, a beauty salon, and other fancy touches. Some master bedrooms had two double beds and a shower! The kitchen served fabulous four- or five-course dinners in luxurious surroundings. These limiteds didn't really make much money because they cost so much to run. But they looked good, and they were great advertising for the railroad.

※ LIFE INSIDE THE TERMINAL ※

Grand Central Terminal was a lively place. The Main Concourse had become the city's unofficial town square—home to all sorts of special events and the setting for some amazing scenes. Have you ever heard the old story about selling the Brooklyn Bridge to some gullible person for a dollar? Here's a similar tale—and it's true.

In 1929 a couple of con men actually collected $10,000 from two brothers who thought they'd just bought the information booth in the Main Concourse. The brothers

Left: Passengers on the 20th Century Limited eat gourmet meals in the elegant dining car. Right: The actress Evelyn Nichols waves from the observation platform, circa 1924. Below: People still meet at the information booth in the Main Concourse, under one of the world's most famous clocks.

36

Elephant boy had to force charge to knees so animal could be squeezed through a taxi ramp

A cartoon from a magazine makes fun of how the elephants had to crawl out of Grand Central Terminal.

were going to use it for a fruit stand—after they enlarged it a little. You can imagine their surprise when they showed up one morning with carpenters and lumber, only to learn that they'd been had. The brothers never did get their money back, and the police never got the con men, who probably caught the next train out of town.

The terminal has had its share of animal stories as well. One involved an arriving circus train that contained, among other things, two elephants. The circus's arrival went smoothly until it was discovered that none of the exits were large enough to get the elephants out. Panic ensued! Trainers finally had to coax them down on to their knees near an exit to the taxi ramp. The elephants were then cajoled out the exit on their stomachs—and calm was restored.

On one unforgettable day, 35 police officers from Los Angeles, in town for a convention, made novel use of the station's ramps. With sirens blaring, they came thundering out of their train's baggage car on motorcycles, shot up the platform, through the Main Concourse, up the ramps, and out on to 42nd Street. Even New Yorkers who thought they'd seen everything were stopped in their tracks.

❋ THE END OF GLORY ❋

On July 3, 1947, a record 252,251 passengers used the terminal. But shortly thereafter, the glory days of railroading came to an end. The rich and famous—and most everyone else—began using airplanes for long-distance travel. The government built new highways, and more people bought cars. Freight traveled on trucks. And although commuters still used the terminal, the railroad was losing over $20 million a year.

The walls and ceilings of the terminal were dirty and peeling.

As the railroad went, so went the terminal. Lack of money led to neglect, which led to dirt, disrepair, and a leaky roof. Desperate for money, the railroad began to allow hideous advertising displays in the Main Concourse. Huge billboards, kiosks, a brokerage office, and enormous new car displays turned the terminal into a "billboard jungle."

Over in the Main Waiting Room, no one was waiting—at least not for trains. Since people now took planes for long-distance trips, there was little to wait for in the terminal. So the homeless moved in. The once-serene space turned into a 24-hour scene, boisterous and dangerous. Bathrooms were filthy and unsafe. Windows were too crusty with grime for any sunlight to penetrate. The carved benches were removed to discourage loitering. It became a scary place.

Broken water fountains were used as trash bins–and worse.

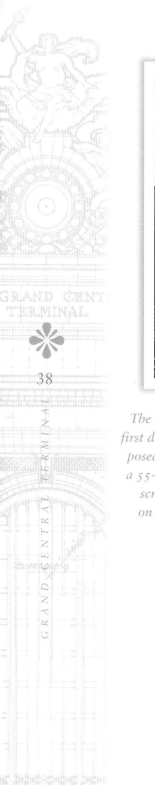

The architect's first design proposed building a 55-story skyscraper right on top of the terminal.

In desperation the railroad closed the terminal between the hours of 1:30 and 5:00 A.M. to discourage drifters. Never in 60 years had the terminal closed—until now. And then came the worst threat of all.

Remember air rights? Still looking for ways to make money, the railroad took a look at the empty space over Grand Central Terminal and saw dollar signs. Why maintain an outdated, squat, five-story building when a modern skyscraper could rise there? A skyscraper's tenants would pay a lot of rent. So even though the terminal had been designated a landmark in 1967, the railroad forged ahead with the plan to build.

In 1968 a respected architect designed a 55-story skyscraper that would sit right on top of Grand Central. Although it wouldn't have required demolition of the whole terminal, it would have required demolishing the Main Waiting Room and half of the Main Concourse. No way, said the Landmarks Preservation Commission. So back came the architect with second plan. This one would have required total demolition of the façade (but it would have saved the Concourse, more or less).

This plan was denied as well, and the battle was on. It seemed there was no way to lease the air rights without destroying the terminal. But the railroad wanted those profits—so it went to court to get them.

GRAND CENTRAL TERMINAL

WAS FIGHTING FOR ITS LIFE.

CHAPTER SIX

A TRAIN STATION FOR THE 21ST CENTURY

✳ COMING TO THE RESCUE ✳

THE RAILROAD TOOK its fight all the way to the U.S. Supreme Court. Because they could not build a skyscraper using the air rights, the railroad felt that the Landmarks Preservation Law was taking away both their property—even though the property was only air—and the income that "property" could produce in the form of rent. They argued that if New York wanted to keep Grand Central as it was, the city should then pay the railroad back for the "property" and income they were taking away.

Meanwhile, New Yorkers were getting involved—people who cared about historic buildings and, especially, people who loved the terminal. The Committee to Save Grand Central had been formed in 1975—a determined band of citizens who refused to give up. Some celebrities joined the group as well. Perhaps the most famous was former first lady Jacqueline Kennedy Onassis, who read a newspaper article about the fight to save Grand Central, picked up the phone, and offered to help. "Old buildings are important," she said. "If we don't care about our past, we cannot

The Committee to Save Grand Central sponsored performances in the terminal to raise public awareness of its cause.

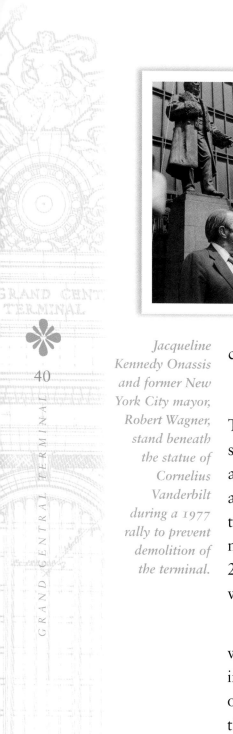

Jacqueline Kennedy Onassis and former New York City mayor, Robert Wagner, stand beneath the statue of Cornelius Vanderbilt during a 1977 rally to prevent demolition of the terminal.

hope for our future." Many people believe that without her hard work and dedication, the terminal might not have survived.

But survive it did. In a historic decision, on June 26, 1978, the Supreme Court ruled in favor of the Landmarks Preservation Commission—and in favor of Grand Central. In New York and all across the country, people celebrated that decision. But the fight wasn't over.

✳ A FRAGILE LANDMARK ✳

The threat of the wrecking ball was gone, for now. But Grand Central still needed saving—from years of neglect. And that would require a great deal of money. The terminal needed to do more than sit as a monument to the past—it needed a future. So the railroad decided to commission a master plan that would describe that future. People needed to know that Grand Central would be an important part of the 21st century as well as the 20th. Then they could support the effort with their hearts and minds—and checkbooks.

The architectural firm that had done the restoration of Ellis Island was chosen to care for Grand Central as well. Their job had two important focuses: to understand and respect Whitney Warren's original intentions, and to create a terminal for changing times and for the needs of the 500,000 people who came there every day. Sound easy? It wasn't.

✳ BUILDING EXCITEMENT ✳

The architects felt it was important to get as many users of the terminal excited about their plan as possible. First, workers took down the huge billboard that had been blocking the three windows on one balcony of the Main Concourse since 1950. They worked behind a

curtain so no one would know what was happening. Once the billboard was removed, they took down the curtain and stood by to watch the reaction. Commuters were speechless. Excitement grew.

Then the architects did something maybe even more effective. They put up a scaffold in one corner of the vaulted ceiling of the Main Concourse, set up a black net to conceal their work, and carefully cleaned a 75-foot-long (23 m) patch of ceiling and moldings. When the net was removed, it looked like a beam of light was shining onto that patch of ceiling. But it was no beam of light. This idea got just the reaction the architects had hoped for. The government agreed to provide almost $3 million for restoration of the ceiling.

In 1994 the master plan was completed and approved—and the real work began.

When the billboard that had been blocking part of the magnificent windows was removed, the Main Concourse was bathed in new light.

✻ GETTING STARTED ✻

Because it was in such dreadful shape, the Main Waiting Room seemed like a good place to begin. Workers felt they could use it almost like a lab, experimenting to see what techniques and materials would work best on the rest of the terminal. Carefully they lowered and took apart the five chandeliers and sent them out to Utah to be restored. They tested paint and found new sources of marble. One quarry in Tennessee was actually reopened to supply marble for the floors and a new staircase.

What appears to be a beam of light shining on the ceiling is actually a cleaned patch, with decades of dirt removed.

Toughest of all was the artificial stone wall. Most methods of cleaning just pushed the dirt further in. So workers did just the opposite. They coated the walls with liquid rubber and let it dry overnight. When they peeled it off in the morning, all the grease and grime came with it. After 18 months the newly renamed Vanderbilt Hall was ready for special events. A particularly special one took place in 1994, when Jacqueline Kennedy Onassis, who had died earlier that year, was remembered at a memorial service—right within the walls she had worked so hard to save.

❋ RESTORING THE CEILING...AND MORE ❋

Cleaning the celestial ceiling at first seemed daunting—but the solution turned out to be pretty basic. Mostly soap and water. All work had to be done while the Concourse was in use, which meant about 500,000 people a day walking beneath the ceiling. It would be important to protect them from falling debris. Remember the train shed? Workers dismantling its glass roof had a similar problem—and a similar solution! Once again a traveling platform was built on top of a scaffold that moved on wheels. The wheels still rested on tracks, but this time the tracks were 100 feet (30.5 m) in the air.

one of the ceiling's 2,500 stars, half-cleaned

As one strip of ceiling was restored, the platform was rolled ahead to the next strip. Soon, people looking up could see the restored ceiling on one side of the platform and the grimy one on the other. They were transfixed by what they saw. Today you can still see one lone unrestored spot—left just as it was, lest we forget.

The architects made two major changes to the Concourse, but only after discovering that these changes were, in fact, exactly what Whitney Warren had in mind in the first place! They removed an old ticket office expansion from 1927 that had created a claustrophobic ceiling over the ramps. Once again, commuters were stopped in their tracks by the new vistas that opened up. The architects also created a grand new marble staircase at the eastern end of the Concourse—one that was in Warren's original plans but never built.

And remember the eagles? One of them—found hidden in shrubbery in upstate New York—came home to roost, right over a new entrance to the terminal.

Above: A traveling platform allowed workers to clean the ceiling without injuring people using the terminal or disrupting service. *Below:* An eagle from the 1898 Grand Central makes its way through the Main Concourse en route to its new Lexington Ave. perch.

✳ THE REDEDICATION ✳

In October of 1998 the newly restored Grand Central Terminal was celebrated. Five thousand people came to see a laser light show, hear music, and watch trapeze artists perform in the Main Concourse. But the real star of the show was, of course, the terminal itself—grand once more, in every sense of the word.

The restoration was a complete success. It took ten years—just as long as it took to build the terminal in the first place! New shops and restaurants ensure that Grand Central will be busy at all hours—not just during rush hour. And it is still a place of remarkable movement, both vertical and horizontal, both within the terminal and through it, coming in and going out.

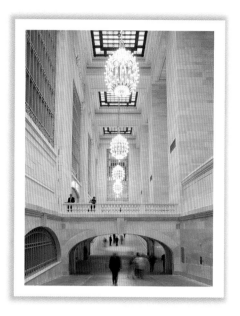

Before restoration (left) the ramp's ceilings were low and the passageways felt claustrophobic. When the lowered floor was removed during restoration (right) the new vistas were breathtaking.

The system of ramps and passageways that first guided travelers in 1913 today gracefully guides a whole new set of travelers with very different destinations. Once again, thousands of lives touch and cross on their way to someplace else.

❋ ❋ ❋

So, the next time you are in New York City, go to 42nd Street at Park Avenue. You'll see a majestic building on the north side of the street. Gaze in awe at the main façade, crowned by sculpture and pierced by triumphal arches. Go in. Follow the ramps or the stairs to the Main Concourse. Look up. Look around. Miraculous, isn't it?

THAT MIRACLE IS
GRAND CENTRAL TERMINAL.

1832 The railroad comes to New York City—NY and Harlem Railroad terminal built on Center Street

1856 Steam locomotives banned south of 42nd Street; trains are decoupled there and pulled by horses down to the terminal

1859 New terminal built at Fourth Avenue and 26th Street

1869 Vanderbilt assembles his railroad empire and begins construction of the first Grand Central

1871 Grand Central Depot opens at Fourth Avenue and 42nd Street

1872–1874 Tracks are placed in an "open cut" from the terminal to 56th Street; tracks are set in a tunnel from 56th to 96th Streets

1877 Vanderbilt dies; train shed roof collapses

1898 Grand Central Station opens (a new façade wrapped around the old depot, which has gained three new floors)

1899 Wilgus begins to ponder electrification of Grand Central; creates initial plan

1900 Interior of Grand Central is reorganized in an attempt to improve traffic flow

1902 Deadly crash in Park Avenue tunnel

1903 Law passed stating that by 1908, the railroad in Manhattan must be electrified

Revised Wilgus plan for all-electric terminal approved by New York City

Architectural competition for design of new terminal; job awarded to Reed & Stem, with the later addition of Warren & Wetmore

Construction begins with track changes and demolition in Bite 1.

1906 First electrified train runs in Grand Central with Wilgus at the controls

1908 Train shed demolished

1910 Old Grand Central Station demolished

1913 New Grand Central Terminal opened to the public

1938 20th Century Limited train begins 16-hour runs between New York and Chicago

1947 Record ridership set

1965 Landmarks Preservation Commission formed in New York City

1967 Exterior of Grand Central Terminal is designated a landmark

First skyscraper over the terminal proposed by railroad

1968 Landmarks Preservation Commission denies proposal

1969 Second skyscraper proposal made by railroad and denied by Landmarks Preservation Committee

1975 Committee to Save Grand Central formed by Municipal Art Society

1978 U.S. Supreme Court upholds landmark status of Grand Central Terminal

1980 Interior of Grand Central Terminal designated a landmark

1988 The architects Beyer Blinder Belle chosen to do the restoration

1990 Master plan presented at public hearing

1994 Final approval of modified master plan

1998 Grand Central Terminal rededicated

air rights the right to build high in the air over the ground you own. Today the air rights over Grand Central Terminal are considered the most valuable real estate in the world.

architect a trained designer of buildings who may also oversee the actual construction or renovation

bedrock the solid rock that lies under all other layers of sand, soil, and gravel. Manhattan bedrock is known for being particularly hard.

bite a series of tasks required to complete a large job. Wilgus divided the project into three bites to allow the railroad to continue operating without any interruptions.

brakeman a member of a train crew who used handbrakes to stop the passenger cars inside the train shed when performing a flying switch

circumferential plaza architect Charles Reed's name for his treatment of Park Avenue, which he wrapped around the new terminal building rather than sending it through the middle. From the word *circumference*—the perimeter of a circle.

civil engineer a person trained to use principles of math and science to design or construct public projects that are efficient and that meet the needs of the public

clockmeister clock repairman

concourse a large hall in a public building; often, the main gathering place

couple to hitch together, as two train cars

curtain wall the exterior wall of a steel-frame building or skyscraper. Curtain walls do nothing to support buildings; they simply hang like curtains to keep weather out and air-conditioned air in.

decouple to unhitch, as two train cars

depot a railroad or bus station

developer someone who builds on real estate (land that is owned as property)

façade the main face of a building

flagman a person who uses flags or other devices for signaling purposes

flying switch a method requiring split-second timing that kept smoky locomotives out of the glass train shed by decoupling them and sending them off to a waiting side track, then quickly throwing the track switch and sending the rest of the train into the shed

Guastavino tile a construction method brought to the U.S. from Spain by Rafael Guastavino in 1881. Guastavino's technique of terra-cotta tiles set in a herringbone pattern enabled him to create self-supporting arches and domes without the need for iron or steel.

head house one of three distinct parts of a railroad terminal, the head house contained waiting and baggage rooms, ticket windows, shops and shoeshine parlors, offices, and newsstands. It did not include the railroad yard or the train shed.

landmark something (usually a building) deemed historically important enough to deserve legal protection from either destruction or alteration

limiteds the long-distance trains that were the ultimate in public transportation for almost 40 years, until about 1950, so-called because they made only limited stops. They arrived and departed with great fanfare.

looping tracks tracks that do not come to a dead end, but which continue around in a loop so that trains may both enter and leave a terminal in a forward direction

master plan an overview of a project that provides a complete description plus overall instructions, goals, and guidance

ramp an inclined plane used to make movement easier or more efficient

semaphore a flag or light used for signaling purposes

signalman a person who operates signal flags and lights (semaphores)

steel-frame construction a building method that uses a framework of structural steel to support a building's floors and walls.

The framework acts as a skeleton for the building. Exterior walls, called curtain walls, do not support anything.

structural steel specially processed steel (actually a combination of steel, iron, carbon, and other elements) that is strong enough to be used to construct such things as bridges, tunnels, and skyscrapers

suburbs residential areas located outside of cities. Frequently people living in a city's suburbs commute by train, bus, or car into the city to work.

technology a way of accomplishing a task using the available technical processes and/or current scientific methods and knowledge

terminal station located at either end of a transportation line

third rail the rail that the electricity runs through that powers trains on electric railroads

towerman a man who watched railroad traffic from a signal tower and conveyed instructions to men operating the track levers and signals

traffic flow the recurring path that traffic naturally takes over time. Traffic can be either vehicular or pedestrian— or a combination of both.